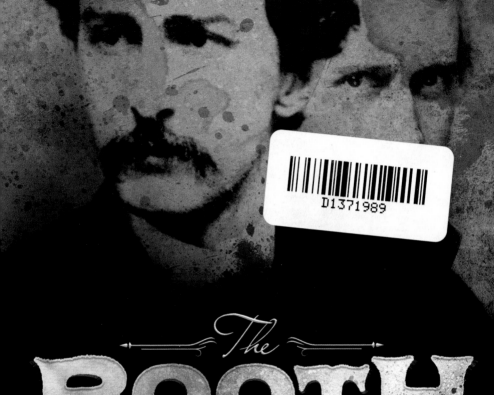

The BOOTH BROTHERS

DRAMA, FAME, AND THE DEATH
OF PRESIDENT LINCOLN

Encounter is published by Capstone Press,
1710 Roe Crest Drive, North Mankato, Minnesota 56003
www.mycapstone.com

Library of Congress Cataloging-in-Publication Data
Names: Langston-George, Rebecca, author.
Title: The Booth brothers : drama, fame, and the death of President Lincoln /
by Rebecca Langston-George.
Description: North Mankato, Minnesota : Capstone, 2018. | Series: Encounter: narrative
nonfiction stories | Includes index.
Identifiers: LCCN 2017004672| ISBN 9781515773382 (library binding) |
ISBN 9781515773399 (paperback) | ISBN 9781515773436 (eBook PDF)
Subjects: LCSH: Booth, John Wilkes, 1838-1865—Juvenile literature. | Booth, John Wilkes,
1838-1865—Family—Juvenile literature. | Booth, Edwin, 1833-1893—Juvenile literature. |
Lincoln, Abraham, 1809-1865—Assassination—Juvenile literature. | Assassins—United States—
Biography—Juvenile literature. | Actors—United States—Biography—Juvenile literature. |
Brothers—United States—Biography—Juvenile literature.
Classification: LCC E457.5 .L25 2018 | DDC 973.70922 [B] —dc23
LC record available at https://lccn.loc.gov/2017004672

Editorial Credits
Nick Healy, editor; Russell Griesmer, designer;
Eric Gohl, media researcher; Tori Abraham, production specialist

Photo Credits

TABLE OF CONTENTS

A WANTED MAN

CHAPTER 1

The cold night sky shrouded the barn in inky darkness. Gusts of chilling wind passed through the slats of the barn walls, rustling the frames used to hang drying tobacco leaves inside. Indeed, it was cold that long-ago morning, April 26, 1865, but the man lying in the hay on the floor dared not risk lighting a fire in the barn's stove. Wounded and weary from travel, his body may have cried out for warmth, but a fire was a chance he did not take. Other, more prudent men might have feared a stray spark would ignite the hay, but he had never been the cautious sort. At the moment, he feared the smoke and light from a fire could bring something more dangerous — the men who were hunting for him.

He had been on the run for 12 days. Along with his companion, David Herold, he had scurried from place to place during that time. Each stop was a hideout. Each host was an accomplice, willing or not. He had a price on his head. Posters all across the country offered a $100,000 reward for the man and his accomplices. He was John Wilkes Booth, the most wanted man in America, and he had committed a crime so heinous there was scarcely a newspaper in the country that hadn't splashed his act across its front page.

To Booth's great surprise, however, the newspapers had not painted him as a hero, as he had anticipated. Certainly, he had not expected praise from Northern papers. But to be declared a criminal in his beloved South was a wound more painful than the fractured leg that had been slowing him down.

John Wilkes Booth had enjoyed a successful career as a
stage actor, but he became consumed by resentment and anger
during the Civil War.

Many miles away, John's older brother Edwin
was in hiding of another sort. Edwin Booth ranked
among the country's best-known actors, and he was
accustomed to seeing his picture in the newspaper. He
was no stranger to being the subject of gossip. But

his brother's actions had put his entire family under criminal suspicion. Their older brother Junius, known as June, and John Clarke, their brother-in-law, had been jailed. They were suspected of helping John Wilkes Booth plan his crime. Edwin's scheduled performances were all canceled. Booth — a last name that had drawn great crowds of paying customers into theaters — had become overnight a lightning rod for hatred, gossip, and threats.

Edwin stayed in seclusion, hoping to avoid both the public and the newspaper reporters. He believed he might be taken into custody at any time. He worried for his mother.

After reading in the newspaper of her brother's crime and then, only minutes later, watching her husband's arrest as a suspected accomplice, his pregnant sister, Asia Clarke, had fallen ill. Surely Edwin, along with the rest of America, wondered where John Wilkes Booth had gone. Had he committed the crime of which he was accused? Had others helped?

Edwin and his family members likely shared one worry that their fellow citizens did not. Was their brother all right?

Feverish and aching in the cold, dark barn, John Wilkes Booth badly needed rest. He knew he would have to move on when the sun rose. Clearly, his latest host, Mr. Richard H. Garrett, had become suspicious. Initially John had passed himself off as a wounded Confederate soldier trying to make his way home. But Booth hadn't played that part effectively. He was too well armed and too eager to reach for his guns when Union soldiers passed by. Also, Garrett's son John had heard that soldiers were scouring the area for an assassin. What would happen if they should find such a man in his guest room? After dinner John Garrett told his guest he was no longer welcome in his house, but he offered to take Booth and Herold elsewhere in the morning.

And so, denied the soft, warm bed he'd enjoyed the last few nights, John lay on a pile of hay in the old tobacco barn with his leg throbbing and his pride wounded. It was after 2 o'clock in the morning when he jerked awake. The sound of horse hooves fell on his ears. The night air came alive with whispers and footsteps. A dim flicker of candlelight bobbed between the barn slats, growing brighter and closer. Union soldiers were coming.

John Wilkes Booth pulled out his revolver. He and David Herold dashed for the barn door. But, fearing Booth and Herold would steal their horses, Garrett and his sons had trapped them. The door was locked on the outside. Furious, Booth and Herold tried kicking some barn slats loose enough to crawl under. But there was no escape for the most wanted man in America. President Abraham Lincoln's murderer had finally been found.

War Department, Washington, April 20, 1865.

$100,000 REWARD!

THE MURDERER

Of our late beloved President, ABRAHAM LINCOLN,

IS STILL AT LARGE.

$50,000 REWARD!

will be paid by this Department for his apprehension, in addition to any reward offered by Municipal Authorities or State Executives.

$25,000 REWARD!

will be paid for the apprehension of JOHN H. SURRATT, one of Booth's accomplices.

$25,000 REWARD!

will be paid for the apprehension of DANIEL C. HARROLD, another of Booth's accomplices.

LIBERAL REWARDS will be paid for any information that shall conduce to the arrest of either of the above-named criminals, or their accomplices.

All persons harboring or secreting the said persons, or either of them, or aiding or assisting their concealment or escape, will be treated as accomplices in the murder of the President and the attempted assassination of the Secretary of State, and shall be subject to trial before a Military Commission and the punishment of DEATH.

Let the stain of innocent blood be removed from the land by the arrest and punishment of the murderers.

All good citizens are exhorted to aid public justice on this occasion. Every man should consider his own conscience charged with this solemn duty, and rest neither night nor day until it be accomplished.

EDWIN M. STANTON, *Secretary of War.*

DESCRIPTIONS.—BOOTH is 5 feet 7 or 8 inches high, slender build, high forehead, black hair, black eyes, and wears a heavy black moustache.

JOHN H. SURRATT is about 5 feet 9 inches. Hair rather thin and dark; eyes rather light; no beard. Would weigh 145 or 150 pounds. Complexion rather pale and clear, with color in his cheeks. Wore light clothes of fine quality. Shoulders square; cheek bones rather prominent; chin narrow; ears projecting at the top; forehead rather low and square, but broad. Parts his hair on the right side; neck rather long. His lips are firmly set. A slim man.

DANIEL C. HARROLD is 23 years of age, 5 feet 6 or 7 inches high, rather broad shouldered, otherwise light built; dark hair, little (if any) moustache; dark eyes; weighs about 140 pounds.

GEO. F. NESBITT & CO., Printers and Stationers, cor. Pearl and Pine Streets, N. Y.

Rewards totaling $100,000 were promised for the capture of John Wilkes Booth and two others involved in the assassination plot. Booth had expected to be a hero in the South, and he was dismayed when even Southern newspapers labeled him a villain.

WITNESS TO HISTORY

CHAPTER 2

Six years earlier, John Wilkes Booth had a different experience with soldiers. He played one — not on the stage but in a real-life drama prior to the Civil War. John, like his two older brothers, had taken up acting. They were all sons of the deceased Shakespearean actor Junius Brutus Booth, and acting ran in the Booth family blood.

During a November 24, 1859, rehearsal at a theater in Richmond, Virginia, for the comedy *Timothy Toodles*, John stepped outside to take a break. The streets were filled with uniformed soldiers waiting to board a train to Charlestown, Virginia. They had been called to duty to maintain order at an execution scheduled for December 2.

The condemned man was John Brown, a radical abolitionist who had been using violent means to fight against slavery. Brown and his followers had tried to gain control of federal weapons stored in the town of Harper's Ferry, Virginia. He planned to arm slaves and lead them in a revolution to abolish slavery. But the plan had been foiled. Brown and six of his followers were captured by soldiers, and Brown was the first sentenced to hang. The governor feared Brown's supporters might show up at the execution to free him by force, so he had called up 1,500 military men to act as guards.

Outside the Richmond theater, John Wilkes Booth struck up a conversation with the waiting soldiers. Upon hearing their destination, Booth was eager to join them. He claimed he wanted to find out what it felt like to be a soldier. Given his political beliefs, he may also have been keen to see an abolitionist swing by the neck.

Soldiers from the Richmond Grays gathered at the execution of
John Brown, a crusader who turned to violence in his effort
to abolish slavery in the United States.

Someone provided him with a gray Richmond

militia uniform. To the delight of the soldiers, the

young actor boarded the train and joined them on their

journey. When the other soldiers asked who would take

his place on stage that night, Booth said he neither

knew nor cared. John Wilkes Booth was relishing the rank of make-believe private.

His skills as an actor served him well as he camped with his new military acquaintances. For their amusement, he spent each evening reciting dramatic poems and bits and pieces of plays. John was so engaging and charming that a reporter there to cover the execution even wrote a story about him for the *Richmond Enquirer* newspaper. "Amongst them I notice Mr. J. Wilkes Booth, a son of Junius Brutus Booth, who, though not a member, as soon as he heard the tap of the drum . . . shouldered his musket and marched with the Grays."

Far away from Charlestown, Edwin Booth's fiancée, Mary Devlin, didn't share the reporter's admiration for her future brother-in-law. Replying to Edwin's letter describing his brother's action, she wrote, "Your news concerning the mad step John has taken I confess did not surprise me. 'Tis a great pity he has not more sense but time will teach him . . ."

While John entertained troops and played soldier, Edwin Booth had begun to settle down into a stable life — at least, a life as stable as an actor could have at the time. He traveled most of the year, performing Shakespeare like his father before him. As a rising star of the stage, he began to make powerful friends.

One year before the execution of John Brown, 24-year-old Edwin was invited to the home of Dr. Samuel Howe and his wife, Julia Ward Howe. The Howes had just seen him perform at the Boston Theater. Dr. Howe ran a school for the blind, and his wife would soon gain fame for writing the song *The Battle Hymn of the Republic*. They were among Boston's elite social families. They were also dedicated abolitionists. Their home, called Green Peace, had served as a stop on the Underground Railroad. It provided safe harbor for runaway slaves for more than 10 years.

While others in their social circles turned up their noses at the thought of rubbing elbows with common actors, the Howes considered Edwin Booth a great artist of the stage. Julia Howe wrote about him in her diary, "In every word and every gesture, the touch of genius made itself felt." In the fall of 1858, Julia threw the first of several parties in Edwin's honor to introduce the young actor to Boston society. Their friendship would last throughout their lives.

Through the Howes, Edwin Booth's social circle overlapped with John Brown's. The Howes had hosted Brown at their home, and Dr. Howe had met with him on several occasions. He also had introduced Brown to others who shared their views on slavery and politics. The Howes, along with their wealthy friends, provided much of the money Brown needed to arm his supporters and obtain land in Harper's Ferry. In fact, Dr. Howe was one of the "Secret Six," a group of Brown's most reliable financial backers. The Howes, while supporting Brown's abolitionist cause, may have chosen to stay ignorant of the more violent details of Brown's plan.

While one brother rubbed elbows with abolitionists in high society, the other stood guard nearby as the Howes' best hope for fighting slavery was taken from his jail cell.

In Charlestown, John Brown handed his silver watch to his jailer, John Avis, to thank him for his care. Head held high, Brown was led to the back of the wagon that carried him to the gallows. His own coffin, a long wooden box, served as his seat. After he mounted the steps to the execution site, Brown's neck was secured in a noose. Just before his head was shrouded with a white hood, Brown took his last glimpse of this earth. He saw a tight circle of soldiers surrounding him. No armed mob came to free him. The platform under Brown's feet dropped open, and he died by hanging.

John Wilkes Booth later wrote, "I saw John Brown hung. And I blessed the justice of my countrys (sic) laws. I may say I helped to hang John Brown and while I live, I shall think with joy upon the day when I saw the sun go down upon one trator (sic) less within our land."

While Brown did not live to see slavery abolished, he left John Avis a note that would prove prophetic. It read, "I, John Brown, am now quite certain that the crimes of this guilty land will never be purged away, but with Blood. I had . . . vainly flattered myself that without very much bloodshed it might be done."

Just as Brown predicted, blood would indeed flow soon. The first shots of the Civil War, the bloodiest chapter in American history, were mere months away.

Your Friend
John Brown

Many people considered John Brown a hero and crusader against
slavery, while others regarded him as a villain and murderer. He
was 59 years old when he was executed in Virginia.

FAMILY AND COUNTRY DIVIDED

CHAPTER 3

With both brothers walking in their famous father's acting footsteps, another problem had arisen. There wasn't room for two famous Booth actors. Edwin decided they would split the country between them. He would tour the North and its rich urban cities such as New York and Boston. John Wilkes could have the South. Brother Junius, the oldest of the Booths, had settled in California years earlier during the Gold Rush. While he too had taken up acting, there were vast territories of mountains and plains separating him from his young brothers' ambitions.

A deep division between the North and South was brewing in the country as well. Slavery was splitting what were then the 33 states of the United States of America. Fifteen of the states were slave states, allowing people to be bought, sold, and enslaved within their borders. The slave states ran from Maryland all the way down to Florida to the south and Texas to the west. The northern states were known as free states, but even in those places, the laws related to runaway slaves, former slaves, and slaves transported across state lines were often complicated and unfair.

The presidential election of 1860 was especially divisive due to the issue of slavery and states' rights. Some wanted an expansion of slavery and more rights for slave owners. Others wanted slavery outlawed throughout the country. The disagreement led to a split in the Democratic Party, which divided along free and slave states into the Northern Democratic Party and the Southern Democratic Party. A new party called the Constitutional Union Party also formed. This fragmenting of political groups left the Republican Party poised to win.

The Republicans had formed just a few years earlier, in 1854, as a largely anti-slavery party. They had chosen Abraham Lincoln, a lawyer and former congressman from Illinois, as their candidate in 1860.

Lincoln's political view of slavery was well known. Just two years earlier, when he was selected as Illinois' Republican candidate in a U.S. Senate race, Lincoln had delivered a now-famous speech called "A House Divided." In it he said, "A house divided against itself cannot stand. I believe this government cannot endure, permanently, half slave and half free. I do not expect the Union to be dissolved — I do not expect the house to fall — but I do expect it will cease to be divided. It will become all one thing or all the other."

Lincoln lost that Senate election to Stephen A. Douglas. In 1860 Lincoln faced his old rival once more in the presidential election. This time Lincoln triumphed over Douglas and two other candidates to become the 16th president. Many in the South were not pleased, to say the least.

Within days, South Carolina's General Assembly passed a resolution calling Lincoln's election "a hostile act." The following month, in December 1860, South Carolina seceded, or withdrew, from the Union. Other states followed. In February 1861, South Carolina, Florida, Alabama, Mississippi, Georgia, Louisiana,

Abraham Lincoln's victory in the 1860 election sent a shock through the South, where leaders quickly moved to break from the Union.

and Texas joined together to create the Confederate States of America. Even before Lincoln was sworn in, the Confederacy swore in its own president, Jefferson Davis, on February 9, 1861. The U.S. government, however, did not view the Confederacy or its president as legal.

It was over this divided nation on the brink of war that Abraham Lincoln swore his presidential oath on March 4, 1861. In his inaugural address he said to the Confederacy, "In your hand, my fellow countrymen, and not in mine, is the momentous issue of civil war. The government will not assail you. You can have no conflict without being yourselves the aggressors."

Hostilities ran high, turning neighbor against neighbor. The Booth family was no exception. John Wilkes Booth and his siblings had grown up on a family farm in Maryland with slaves leased by their father. John Wilkes Booth considered himself a Southerner. He had no love for Lincoln or his policies limiting states' rights. John's sister Asia described him as "an ardent lover of the South and her policy, an upholder of Southern principles."

Edwin, on the other hand, considered himself a Northerner. He continued to associate with abolitionists and his best friend, Adam Badeau, became a Union soldier. Edwin had little tolerance for his younger brother's rants against Lincoln and his support of slavery.

So the brothers split the country between them. But while John Wilkes did play mostly in the South, he also made appearances in the North, much to Edwin's annoyance. According to his sister Asia, "He (John) felt it rather premature that Edwin should mark off for himself the North and the East, and leave the South where he no longer cared to go himself, to Wilkes."

Edwin Booth posed in costume for his role as the villain
Iago in Shakespeare's *Othello*. Booth earned acclaim by
performing in several of Shakespeare's famed works.

ACTORS AND RIVALS

CHAPTER 4

It didn't take long for John Wilkes Booth's beloved South to take action against the North. After the secession of the Confederate states, Lincoln attempted to keep for the North the forts and armories located within the Confederacy. He stationed soldiers there to secure them. Just 39 days after Lincoln took office, the Confederacy tested Lincoln's resolve. It fired upon Fort Sumter in South Carolina, which was being held by U.S. soldiers under the American flag. With that, the Civil War had begun.

Before long, the Confederacy grew to 11 states with the addition of Virginia, Arkansas, North Carolina, and

Tennessee. For four years the battle raged, tearing the country apart and snuffing out the lives of young men drafted to serve. Modern historians believe more than 752,000 people lost their lives during the Civil War.

John Wilkes Booth and his brother Edwin quietly fought their own battles during the Civil War. Each billed himself as the son of Junius Brutus Booth, the famous tragedian. Each worked to show the public their father had passed the torch on to him.

The Confederate Army fired on U.S. troops at Fort Sumter, near Charleston, South Carolina, on April 12, 1861. Coming little more than a month after Lincoln took office, the bombardment amounted to the first shots of the Civil War.

Edwin Booth had an advantage over his younger brother because he had served as his father's assistant for several years. Beginning at the age of 12, he traveled with his father as he performed across the country. Edwin cared for his father's costumes, wigs, and makeup kit, and listened to him rehearse lines. Although Junius Brutus Booth would not allow his family to watch him perform, Edwin regularly hid backstage to spy between the curtains while his father captivated audiences. He said, "At an early age my memory became stored with the words of all the parts of every play in which my father performed."

In addition to caring for his father's wardrobe, Edwin also had the unpleasant task of being his father's keeper. He steered his father away from saloons and made sure he was sober enough to perform. When payday arrived, Edwin made sure his father did not gamble away the family income. At his father's bidding, Edwin took small parts in his father's plays when he became a teenager. When his father sank into one of his famous depressions, 17-year-old Edwin took his father's place one night in Shakespeare's *Richard III* in New York. When a fellow actor asked Junius Brutus Booth which of his sons would succeed him as an actor, Junius silently laid his hand upon Edwin.

Edwin's younger brother may have felt cheated from an early age since he didn't get to join his father on the road. Like his elder brother, John Wilkes Booth caught the acting bug, but his parents insisted he stay in school. He was also expected to help run the family farm. The flamboyant John Wilkes, however, took to neither studying nor farming. Books and plows brought no joy to the heart that longed for greasepaint, footlights, and thunderous applause.

The Booth brothers' father died at the age of 56, having never taken the eager John Wilkes under his wing as an actor. This did not deter the younger Booth from pursuing the stage. His first parts were small, and his mother joked that his earnings wouldn't even pay for his cigar habit. He used the name J.B. Wilkes at first, as the Booth family thought he should earn a good reputation before using the great Junius Brutus Booth's last name.

While his older brother had received his father's blessing, John Wilkes inherited something else valuable: his father's costumes. The garments had been designed and hand-sewn by his mother, Mary Ann Holmes. She made the decision to pass her late husband's theatrical wardrobe to her favorite son, John Wilkes. This, no doubt, did not sit well with Edwin, who had spent years of his life cleaning, pressing, mending, and fastening his father into those same costumes.

Of the two brothers, John Wilkes most closely resembled their famous father. Not only did John Wilkes look like the famous performer, his approach to acting was eerily similar to his father's larger-than-life style. He was loud. His gestures were broad and wild. His fight scenes were so athletic and vivid he often injured himself or his fellow actors. The actress Catherine Winslow, who appeared as Juliet to his Romeo, had some rough encounters with John Wilkes on stage. He once got the buttons of his sleeve tangled in her hair, stood on the hem of her dress (ripping it), and swung her right out of her shoes.

Although John had never seen his father on stage, critics and theater managers certainly saw the similarities. His hometown newspaper, *The Baltimore Sun*, billed him as "The Hope of the American Stage." The advertisement read, "As Pescara . . . an effort of this youthful Baltimore Artist which rivals in its Terrible Intensity the Fame of his Father THE GREAT BOOTH." The newspaper even reprinted a review of his father's performance in the same role from 20 years earlier.

Edwin, on the other hand, developed a style all his own over the years. Unlike his brother, who stormed and stomped across the stage, Edwin relied on his quiet, melodic voice to breathe life into Shakespeare. He spoke as a poet, his voice rising and falling like the ebb of the tide, giving meaning to each phrase. Adam Badeau, critic for the *Sunday Times*, wrote to Edwin after seeing him perform, offering to help him further refine his performances. The two became close friends, with Badeau coaching the man he considered a genius.

Other critics also took notice of Edwin and his work. *The Cincinnati Daily Press* ran an article on Edwin's overseas engagements in 1861. "Mr. Edwin Booth, it is known, is a young man who has displayed prodigious abilities as an actor. Old Shakespearian critics . . . have said . . . there had been no better interpreter of the . . . great bard. He always fills the house with the most refined and intellectual people." The Cincinnati paper also described his readings as "beautiful" and "chaste."

President Abraham Lincoln and his wife, Mary Todd Lincoln, were enthusiastic theatergoers and watched both Booths perform. The Lincoln family saw Edwin

Booth at Grover's National Theater in Washington, D.C., six times. One visit was arranged by theater owner Leonard Grover in honor of the third anniversary of Lincoln's inauguration. President Lincoln himself requested Edwin perform *Hamlet* for him in March 1863. They later saw John Wilkes on stage in *The Marble Heart* on November 9, 1863. That performance took place at Ford's Theatre.

The Lincolns' next encounter with John Wilkes Booth at Ford's Theatre would be deadly.

John Wilkes Booth performed at Ford's Theatre in
Washington, D.C. In *The Marble Heart*, he played a sculptor
who brought his statues to life.

PLANS AND PLOTS

CHAPTER 5

On September 22, 1862, Abraham Lincoln gave the Confederacy a deadline. If it did not surrender by January 1, he would sign a document putting an end to slavery within the Confederate states. The two Booth brothers had very different reactions to the announcement. Edwin Booth organized several plays to benefit charities serving the widows and orphans of Union soldiers. John Wilkes Booth, on the other hand, toyed with the idea of violence. "What a glorious opportunity there is for a man to immortalize himself by killing Lincoln!" he reportedly said in the company of some fellow actors discussing the matter in a Chicago bar that December.

The Confederate States of America turned a deaf ear to Lincoln's demand. On New Year's Day 1863, President Abraham Lincoln signed the Emancipation Proclamation, declaring all slaves in the Confederate states free. "That on the first day of January, in the year of our Lord, one thousand eight hundred and sixty-three, all persons held as slaves within any state or designated part of a state, the people whereof shall then be in rebellion against the United States, shall be then, thenceforward, and forever free . . ."

The document allowed willing slaves to join the U.S. military, which would swell the ranks of the Union Army. But since the Confederacy did not recognize Lincoln's right to govern them, the rebel states simply ignored the proclamation. Lincoln's action had little immediate effect on the lives of slaves. However, Lincoln knew that if states returned to the Union in the future, the Emancipation Proclamation would take effect.

Lincoln upon signing the Emancipation Proclamation

The war raged on with scarcely a pause. While most of the battles were fought in the South, by the middle of 1863, Confederate General Robert E. Lee decided to take the battle to the North. Union and Confederate soldiers met at Gettysburg, Pennsylvania, in the early days of July, and battled fiercely during the three bloodiest days in American history. The two sides combined lost more than 51,000 troops.

Edwin and John Wilkes Booth saw battles of a different sort right outside Edwin's New York home just days later. Edwin, still in mourning at his home after the death of his wife, Mary, allowed John to stay with him for the summer. On Monday, July 13, 1863, the New York Draft Riots broke out close to Edwin's home. For five days violence and chaos erupted all around them.

Men filled the street, shouting and marching to protest the draft, which required males between 20 and 45 to serve as Union soldiers. Only those able to pay the government $300 or hire someone to take their places were excused from the draft. The city's poor, especially the Irish immigrants, considered this unfair. To them, $300 was a great sum of money, and most people didn't have it or couldn't spare it.

Anger and resentment about the draft had reached the boiling point in New York City. Mobs burned and looted shops and other businesses, leaving empty, blackened shells where neighborhood stores once stood. Police officers, trying to stop the violence, were brutally clubbed or axed by the angry rioters.

Before long the anger turned toward those the mob saw as Lincoln supporters: black men and Union soldiers. Vigilantes went door to door, dragging out men in uniform and people of color. Unknown to the mob outside, Edwin Booth was harboring both inside his home. His friend Adam Badeau had come to Edwin's home to recover from a war injury and had brought with him a black attendant to care for his wounds. Edwin sheltered them in his home as the mob lynched men and hung them in trees lining the streets. Their beaten, broken bodies were left there as a warning to others.

Just as the draft incited violence in the streets, the Emancipation Proclamation and the continued war inflamed John Wilkes Booth. When John criticized Lincoln and the North and declared, "My soul, life and possessions are for the South," his siblings asked why John didn't join up and fight for the South. He replied, "My brains are worth twenty men, my money worth a hundred. I have free pass everywhere. My profession, my name, is my passport. My knowledge of drugs is valuable, my beloved precious money — oh, never beloved till now! — is the means, one of the means, by which I serve the South."

His sister, Asia, curious about his mention of drugs, asked why someone had come around asking for "Dr. Booth." John admitted, "I am he, if to be a doctor means a dealer in quinine." Under the cover of his work as a traveling actor, John transported the fever and malaria drug quinine from New York into the South. He hid it inside "horse-collars and so forth."

Breaking the blockade to deliver goods to the South was a crime, but John not only wasn't concerned, he soon set his sights on a much bigger crime. He began planning to kidnap the president.

On October 18, 1864, John Wilkes Booth went to Montreal, Canada, which had become the favorite spot for the Confederate States of America to conduct banking business. He received $300 in gold along with more than $1,000 in cash from the Confederacy's chief banker. He also met with George Sanders, likely a Confederate secret agent. The Confederacy gave him a letter of introduction to present to Southern sympathizers in order to gain their assistance. Neither Booth nor Sanders recorded what they discussed, but some historians suggest Sanders may have planted ideas of kidnapping or assassination in Booth's head on behalf of the Confederacy.

To pull off his scheme, Booth recruited some friends and admirers who shared his political views.

John Wilkes Booth and his associates hatched a plan to kidnap President Lincoln.

Together, they intended to kidnap the president and transport him out of the capital. The group included John Surratt, who was a blockade runner like John Wilkes Booth, as well as a Confederate spy, and several other men. David Herold knew Maryland's back roads and could act as a guide. Lewis Powell was a veteran Confederate soldier. Samuel Arnold and Michael O'Laughlen had been Booth's friends since their school days. George Atzerodt was asked to arrange boats so Booth could ferry the captive president across the water and out of the capital.

The would-be kidnappers held meetings at the boardinghouse run by Surratt's mother, Mary. Booth supplied the alcohol and cigars for the gatherings as he laid out his plans. They would merely need to read the newspapers to find a dinner, play, or event Lincoln would be attending. Perhaps they could catch him en route to the summer residence the president sometimes used. They would lie in wait for his carriage to pass, knock out the driver, and drag Lincoln away to Richmond, the Confederate capital. By holding the president hostage, Booth thought he could negotiate the release of Confederate prisoners of war.

The conspirators surveyed back roads and waterways they might use to spirit Lincoln away. They purchased weapons, handcuffs, horses, and boats to pull off their kidnapping plan. Plotting against

Lucy Lambert Hale, the love interest of John Wilkes Booth

Lincoln consumed John Wilkes Booth's money and his attention. He no longer had time for an actor's life of travel, rehearsals, and late nights at the theater. He told friends and family he had tired of the stage and had taken up oil speculation.

Despite the burdens his complicated secret life put upon him, John Wilkes Booth managed to find time for one of his favorite pursuits: women. The handsome, athletic Booth had always enjoyed the attention of swooning young female fans. He exchanged letters with several women, and to adoring admirers he sent his dark-eyed, bushy-mustached picture. The same mind that contemplated the best method of political kidnapping also concocted poetry for his latest love, Lucy Lambert Hale. His brother June said, "John sat up all Monday night to put Miss H's Valentine in the mail . . . he wrote her a long letter — kept me awake by every now and then using me as a Dictionary."

Lucy was the daughter of a New Hampshire abolitionist senator, making her an odd choice for a man dedicated to the South. Her parents did not think much of the young actor wooing their daughter. They would have preferred that Lucy turn her attention to another possible suitor: Robert Todd Lincoln, an officer in the Union army. That the president's son had shown an interest in Lucy and sent her flowers delighted the Hales — all of them, that is, except for Lucy.

Coincidentally, John Wilkes Booth had his brother Edwin to blame for his possible rival's attention toward his beloved Lucy. In fact, he could probably blame Edwin for Robert Lincoln's very life. Why? Because once Edwin Booth had saved the life of Abraham Lincoln's oldest son.

When traveling through the Jersey City, New Jersey, train station not long after his wife's death, Edwin Booth noticed a young man waiting for the train just as he was bumped off his feet by the huge pressing crowd. The young man fell from the platform onto the rails as a train approached. Edwin reached down and yanked him up by his coat, narrowly preventing his being hit. The younger man recognized the famous actor, thanked him, and said, "That was a close call, Mr. Booth."

Edwin had no idea of the identity of the young man he saved. But later word spread around Washington, D.C., of Robert Lincoln's close encounter with the actor Edwin Booth, who had saved his life. The story eventually became part of the lore surrounding the crime of Edwin's younger brother.

Robert T. Lincoln as photographed in the early 1860s

A COUNTRY REUNITED

CHAPTER 6

By late summer 1864, Edwin Booth and other Union supporters felt their spirits lifted by developments in the war. The North, it seemed, had the upper hand. A key turning point in the Civil War occurred September 2, 1864, when the city of Atlanta, Georgia, fell to the Union Army under Major General William T. Sherman. Sherman's troops had battled with the Confederates through most of the summer before cutting off their supply lines and forcing them to flee. Atlanta, a transportation hub and important industrial city, then fell under Union control.

Union Major General William Tecumseh Sherman

With Northern voters heartened by news of battlefield victories, Abraham Lincoln won a second term as president on November 8, 1864. Edwin proudly cast the only ballot of his life and voted for Lincoln. On November 11, 1864, he wrote to Emma Cary, the widow of a close friend, "I voted (for Lincoln) t' other day — the first vote I ever cast: and I suppose I am now an American citizen all over, as I have ever been in heart."

He also told Mrs. Cary that "On Friday, the 25th, without fail, the long-talked-of benefit 'to Shakespeare' will take place at the Winter Garden, with the 'Brothers Booth' . . . and beginning on the following night Hamlet, in a new dress, will fret his brief hour every night until further notice." The benefit for Shakespeare was a project Edwin had worked on for months. He planned for all three sons of the legendary Junius Brutus Booth to unite for a single night on November 25, 1864, to perform Shakespeare's *Julius Caesar*. The money raised would be used to erect a statue of Shakespeare in New York's Central Park in honor of the 300th anniversary of the writer's birth. *The New York Times* ran a special announcement of the event that day:

> . . . *Owing to the generous zeal and untiring devotion of Mr. Edwin Booth, a performance will be given at this theater on Friday evening, November 25 . . . for the benefit*

of the fund to raise a statue to Shakspeare (sic) *in the Central Park . . . The evening will be made memorable by the appearance in the same piece of the three sons of the great Booth. Junius Brutus, Edwin and John Wilkes, who have come forward in cheerful alacrity to do honor to the immortal bard from whose works the genius of their father caught its inception.*

June appeared as Cassius, Edwin as Brutus, the chief assassin of Julius Caesar, and John Wilkes played Marc Antony.

The show was well received and the three toga-clad brothers walked on stage together at the end to bow to their mother, Mary Ann Holmes. However, the play did not go off exactly as planned. Partway through the performance, the doors burst open and firemen rushed through the lobby to gain access to the LaFarge Hotel next door. It was one of several fires set throughout New York City hotels that night by Confederate secret agents hoping to terrify New Yorkers.

The subject of the fires caused a huge rift between the recently reunited Edwin and John the following Sunday morning. John felt the fires were justified acts of war. He saw no problem with using terrorism against the citizens of the North as revenge for injuries suffered by the South. Edwin exploded, calling his younger brother's words treasonous and telling him he would be thrown out of the house if he continued to bring up the subject. John refused to stay silent and was told to pack his bags.

Edwin Booth began the first of his 100-night run of performances of *Hamlet* the day after the Shakespeare benefit. From November 26, 1864, to March 22, 1865, he performed as Prince Hamlet every night at the Winter Garden Theater. It was an astonishing accomplishment in a time when actors rarely played for more than a few nights at a time in one place. To play the same role night after night in the same theater was unheard of.

John Wilkes Booth made his way to Washington, D.C., where the new year ushered in many changes.

On January 31, 1865, the U.S. Congress passed the 13th Amendment to the Constitution. It stated, "Neither slavery nor involuntary servitude, except as a punishment for crime whereof the party shall have been duly convicted, shall exist within the United States, or any place subject to their jurisdiction." The newly passed 13th Amendment went further than the earlier

John Wilkes Booth reportedly joined the crowd to hear Lincoln's second inaugural address. (Lincoln is visible behind the white lectern at center in this photograph.)

Emancipation Proclamation by outlawing the practice of slavery altogether.

On March 4, 1865, President Abraham Lincoln was inaugurated president for his second term in office. The war-weary president said in his inaugural address, "Fondly do we hope, fervently do we pray, that this mighty scourge of war may speedily pass away."

A mere stone's throw from the president stood John Wilkes Booth, wearing a top hat and likely in a bitter mood. He occupied a spot near the crowded stairs leading down to the platform of the East Front of the Capitol, where Lincoln laid his hand on the Bible and swore his presidential oath. The highly prized ticket for the event had been a gift from Lucy Hale to her sweetheart. Some historians say Booth escorted Lucy Hale to the president's inaugural ball that night. If so, the couple no doubt danced and lifted glasses in the president's honor. Despite the patriotic ceremony, rousing speech, and celebratory ball with his sweetheart by his side, John Wilkes Booth had murder on his mind. "What an excellent chance I had to kill the President on inauguration day if I wished," he later bragged.

A few days later John rented the best private box at Ford's Theatre for his fellow conspirators John Surratt and Lewis Powell, as well as their dates. The price was much higher than regular seats, but the luxury could not be chalked up to Booth's generosity. It was the same box that President Lincoln had sat in on two occasions in the previous month. The president had come to see Booth's brother-in-law, John Sleeper Clarke, perform. This inspired Booth's latest plan.

After the play, Surratt and Powell dismissed their dates and met Booth and others for dinner. Booth proposed that the next time Lincoln occupied the theater box at Ford's they shut down the lights, which would plunge the theater into total darkness. In the darkness they would use chloroform to render Lincoln helpless, carry him down the stairs, and kidnap him.

Edmund Spangler, a stagehand and carpenter at Ford's Theatre, would be willing to take care of the lights. But Booth's fellow plotters argued they weren't likely to succeed with a large audience in the building.

The conspirators again took up the idea of snatching Lincoln from the road. Just days after their visit to the theater, they staked out the quiet country road leading to Campbell Hospital outside Washington, D.C. They had heard the president would be joining the wounded soldiers there to view a play. But Lincoln did not show up. He had changed his plans. Once again, the group's plans were thwarted. It was the last straw for some of his conspirators, who now believed they would never be able to pull off their scheme.

Just days before Edwin's 100th performance of *Hamlet*, John Wilkes Booth took to the stage for the last time. On March 18, 1865, he walked on stage at Ford's Theatre to act as Pescara in *The Apostate*. The sight of the box Lincoln had recently occupied, no doubt, weighed heavily upon his mind.

His brother Edwin, however, was in much better spirits despite his grueling schedule. He had found love once again after years spent in mourning for his first wife, Mary. He and Blanche Hanel were discussing marriage.

Unity was within reach for the long-divided nation as well. The South lost its hold on Richmond, the Confederate capital. On April 2, 1865, Jefferson Davis, along with much of the city's population, fled the capital as Union troops approached. On April 9, 1865, Confederate General Robert E. Lee surrendered his 28,000 troops to Union General Ulysses S. Grant at Appomattox Court House, Virginia. In exchange for laying down their arms, Grant pardoned Lee's men. They were fed and allowed to keep their personal property, including their horses and private weapons. While scattered skirmishes continued for a few weeks,

Lee's surrender effectively ended the Civil War. North and South were once again united.

Celebrations erupted across the nation's capital on April 10, 1865, which became known as Illumination Night. Bands played "Yankee Doodle Dandy" while cheering citizens paraded through the streets, laughing and waving the Stars and Stripes. Candles and gaslights filled windows, illuminating the night while red, white, and blue fireworks burst across the dark sky. Crowds gathered on the lawn of the White House and called for the president to come out. After speaking a few words, he instructed the band to play "Dixie," considered the South's anthem. The celebration spilled over into the next day, and Lincoln was once again urged to appear and speak. Everyone was jubilant. Everyone except for John Wilkes Booth, who stood with the celebrating crowd on the White House lawn and declared to Lewis Powell, "That is the last speech he will ever give."

A NEW PLAN
EXECUTED

CHAPTER 7

On the morning of April 14, 1865, a messenger arrived at Ford's Theatre. First Lady Mary Todd Lincoln had sent word that she and the president, as well as General Grant and his wife, would attend that night's performance of *Our American Cousin*. It was Good Friday, a day on the Christian calendar for reflecting upon the crucifixion and death of Jesus Christ.

John Wilkes Booth came by Ford's Theatre a few hours later and heard the news. The president and the general responsible for the South's defeat were coming to sit in the very box he had directed Surratt and Powell to examine. A plan began to take shape in his mind. A very big plan. He would avenge the South and force the North to its knees by taking out four of its leaders.

As John Wilkes Booth plotted, his brother Edwin, fresh from the success of 100 nights of playing Hamlet, rested at the home of a friend in Boston. Later that evening he was scheduled to star in *The Iron Chest* at the Boston Theater. He never suspected it would be his last performance for months.

After arranging for a horse he intended to use later, John Wilkes Booth walked to the National Hotel where he was staying and asked the clerk for writing paper. He was admitted into the hotel's office, where he wrote a letter to the editor of the *National Intelligencer* newspaper. In it, he explained his reasons for the action he was about to take:

To My Countrymen: For years I have devoted my time, my energies, and every dollar I possessed to the furtherance of an object. I have been baffled and disappointed. The hour has come when I must change my plan. Many, I know —the vulgar herd — will blame me for what I am about to do, but posterity, I am sure, will justify me. Right or wrong,

God judge me, not man.

He ended the rambling letter with a reference to Brutus assassinating Caesar from the very play in which he and his brothers had recently appeared:

When Caesar had conquered the enemies of Rome and the power that was his menaced the liberties of the people, Brutus arose and slew him. The stroke of his dagger was guided by his love of Rome. It was the spirit and ambition of Caesar that Brutus struck at. "Oh that we could come by Caesar's spirit, and not dismember Caesar! But alas! Caesar must bleed for it."

Booth placed the letter in an envelope and asked John Matthews, an actor who would perform that night at Ford's, if he would hold the letter for him and deliver it to the newspaper in the event Booth didn't ask for it back by 10 a.m. the next day. Matthews put the letter in his pocket.

Booth's next errand was at the vice president's residence. Vice President Andrew Johnson lived at a hotel called Kirkwood House. Booth left a visiting card for Johnson with this note: "Don't wish to disturb you; are you at home?" The vice president did not respond. Perhaps Booth wanted to know if he was in town, as Booth had decided to add Johnson to his hit list.

David Herold, a friend of John Wilkes Booth and conspirator in the assassination of President Lincoln

Next he went to Mrs. Surratt's boardinghouse. He gave her a package and instructions related to weapons and supplies he would pick up at her tavern in Surrattsville, Maryland, several miles away. That night he met with George Atzerodt, Lewis Powell, and David Herold a couple of hours before the curtain rose at Ford's Theatre. The plan was to strike President Lincoln, General Grant, Vice President Johnson, and Secretary of State William Seward. The killings would take place across the city during the 10 p.m. hour.

At the appointed hour that evening, George Atzerodt, who was armed with a knife and a six-shooter, entered the Kirkwood House. He had taken a room on the floor above Vice President Johnson's. But Atzerodt did not go to Johnson's room as intended — or to his own room. Instead he sat at the bar and drank. He lost his nerve and couldn't do the deed. Half-drunk, he left the hotel as Vice President Johnson slept soundly a few doors away.

Lewis Powell and David Herold watched Seward's house on Madison Place. The secretary of state had been in a horse carriage accident a few days earlier and had round-the-clock care at his home. At 10 p.m. Powell handed Herold the reins to his horse, went to the door, and rang the bell.

When the servant answered, Powell said he had medicine to deliver and showed the man a small package wrapped in brown paper and string. When the servant offered to take it, Powell insisted he must give it to Seward himself. He bolted up the steps and was met by Frederick Seward, the secretary of state's son, who demanded he leave. Powell tried to shoot him, but his gun misfired. He beat Frederick on the head with the gun, then dashed into Secretary Seward's room, stabbed the secretary of state as well as his nurse, and then battled with Frederick's brother Gus on the way out, stabbing him. David Herold, having heard Seward's daughter Fanny screaming for help out the window, took off before Powell made it out of the bloody house.

General Ulysses S. Grant and his wife, Julia, did not arrive at the theater with the Lincolns that night. They told Mrs. Lincoln they had to go out of town to visit their children in New Jersey. In truth, the Grants had another reason for declining the invitation. Julia Grant did not like Mary Todd Lincoln, and she had recently been on the receiving end of Mrs. Lincoln's acid-tongued remarks. Mrs. Grant's unwillingness to spend the evening in Mrs. Lincoln's company may have saved her husband's life.

Instead, the Lincolns brought Major Henry Rathbone and his fiancée Clara Harris to Ford's Theatre that night. They arrived late, coming in at 8:30 p.m. as the play, *Our American Cousin*, was underway. The audience cheered as the presidential party made its way to the box decorated in red, white, and blue fabric. The actors stopped and the house lights went on so the latecomers could find their seats. Mrs. Lincoln curtsied to the crowd and the president bowed as the orchestra played "Hail to the Chief" in honor of the man who had brought the terrible war to an end. Only after the usher closed the door to the state box and the president motioned for the actors to proceed did the audience become quiet.

John Wilkes Booth retrieved his rented horse, saddled it, and walked it to the alley behind Ford's Theatre. The young man who sold peanuts to theatergoers agreed to hold Booth's horse. Having promised to be back shortly, Booth climbed the stairs to the level that held the state box. At the top of the stairs he quietly opened the door that led to the entrances to the private boxes. Earlier in the day he had planted a small piece of wood along the floor. Now he wedged it across the door to assure no one could push the door open from the outside.

There was one more door to go. It led directly into the state box. Booth leaned against the door and peered through the tiny peephole one of the conspirators had drilled earlier that day. Inside he saw Lincoln sitting in a tall rocking chair. Mrs. Lincoln sat on a chair between him and Clara Harris. Major Rathbone sat on a sofa nearby.

Silently, Booth inched the door open. He drew a deringer pistol from his coat pocket. He aimed the gun at the object of his hatred and pulled the trigger. The gunpowder flashed in the dark box. Wisps of smoke circled near Booth's outstretched arm and the unmistakable smell of burned gunpowder hung in the air. The bullet struck the president below his left ear, entering his brain and leaving him instantly unconscious. Lincoln's head fell forward, and he slumped in the rocking chair.

Shocked by the blast, Major Rathbone stood up to see what had happened. Booth lunged at him with a knife. Rathbone shielded himself, taking a deep cut to his upper arm. Booth pushed past him to the edge of the box and swung his leg over to jump. As he leaped toward the stage, he caught the spur on his boot in the red, white, and blue fabric draped over the outside of the box. This caused him to land badly and injure his leg when he landed 12 feet below on the stage.

The actors on the stage below stood dumbfounded. The assassin turned to face the audience, who were riveted to their seats, unsure if the bizarre scene was all part of the play. Still clutching the blood-spattered

Booth jumped from the president's box after shooting Lincoln and dashed backstage while a stunned and confused audience looked on.

knife, Booth shouted in his best stage voice, "Sic semper tyrannis" (thus always to tyrants), a line often credited to Caesar's assassin, Brutus. Before turning to run, Booth added, "The South is avenged."

Major Rathbone shouted from the state box, "Stop that man!"

Clara Harris yelled, "He has shot the president."

Mrs. Lincoln, clutching her unconscious husband, screamed and wailed.

A HUNTED MAN

CHAPTER 8

In the mass confusion, John Wilkes Booth ran for the stage's back door, brandishing his knife at anyone who came near. He jumped on his horse and galloped out of the back alley, down F Street, and through downtown Washington, D.C.

Inside Ford's Theatre, Laura Keene, the star and producer of *Our American Cousin*, called for calm, shouting over the din from the now crazed audience, "Order, order! Keep your places!"

Major Rathbone, despite his slashed arm, removed the bar Booth had wedged in the box's door to keep it closed. Dr. Leale, a theatergoer who had just graduated from medical school, pushed through the crowd to care for the president. Keene followed him and held the president's head in her lap as Dr. Leale examined him. The young doctor declared, "His wound is mortal. It is impossible for him to recover."

Fearing the president would not survive the trip to the White House, Dr. Leale had Lincoln carried down the stairs and across the street to a boardinghouse opposite the theater.

John Wilkes Booth had to convince a guard to let him cross this bridge, thereby escaping from Washington, D.C., soon after he shot Lincoln.

A bit before 10:45 p.m., John Wilkes Booth arrived at the Navy Yard Bridge linking Washington, D.C., to Maryland. An armed guard stood sentry, with orders to let no one pass after dark. But the charming actor convinced the guard he was merely returning home late. The guard let him pass into Maryland.

David Herold also talked the guard into letting him cross the bridge minutes after Booth passed. The two met up near Soper's Hill, the agreed-upon spot. Lewis Powell was not so lucky. His horse had fled when David Herold ran away, leaving Lewis on the run, quite literally, as he was without transportation.

Booth and Herold stopped at Mary Surratt's tavern, closed for the night. The man who ran the place answered their knock and gave them whiskey and weapons that had been left for them. By this time Booth's broken leg was beginning to throb, and riding a horse aggravated the injury. Then the two traveled to Dr. Samuel Mudd's home, a four-hour ride away.

Mudd was one of the Confederate sympathizers Booth had heard about during his meeting in Canada. Dr. Mudd cut the boot off Booth's injured leg, said the bone was fractured above the ankle, and applied a splint. Knowing nothing of Lincoln's assassination, Dr. Mudd invited the two men to spend the rest of the night in his guest room.

As Booth lay sleeping and Lincoln lay dying, a manhunt for Booth began. Edwin Stanton, the Secretary of War, gave orders to stop people at bridges, search trains, and be on the lookout for the actor who had been identified as Lincoln's assassin by other actors at Ford's Theatre. Booth's room at the National Hotel was searched. Tips that Booth had recently been meeting with John Surratt led to a fruitless search of Mary Surratt's boardinghouse.

President Abraham Lincoln drew his last breath at 7:22 a.m. on the morning of April 15, 1865. Vice President Johnson, who had escaped the assassination plot unhurt, took the presidential oath a few hours later. Secretary of State Seward would eventually recover and serve in Johnson's cabinet.

News of the horrible event soon reached John Wilkes Booth's family and friends. Edwin Booth was awoken that morning by his valet after a late night performing at the Boston Theater. The valet first told him the terrible news of the president's assassination. Then he handed him a newspaper and told him even worse news: Edwin's brother was the prime suspect.

At the National Hotel in Washington, D.C., where soldiers were searching John Wilkes Booth's room, Lucy Hale, whose family was also staying there, came downstairs for breakfast. Upon hearing the news, she screamed and fainted. When John Matthews realized what Booth had done, he opened the letter entrusted to him. Fearing the police would think him part of the plot, he did not give it to the *National Intelligencer*. He burned Booth's letter instead, only to recount it by memory later in the investigation.

By evening, word of Lincoln's death had reached Dr. Mudd. He realized he was harboring fugitives and ordered Herold and Booth to leave. But he also suggested they might find help from Colonel Samuel Cox. They mounted their horses once more, hired a guide, and found their way to Cox's home in Rich Hill, Maryland, on Easter Sunday. While the rest of the nation filled churches across the country to mourn the loss of their president, John Wilkes Booth and David Herold hunkered down in a swampy grove of trees near Cox's home to hide. Each morning Cox sent them food and, at Booth's request, Washington newspapers.

Cold, in pain, and with nothing but leaves and moss for a bed, Booth read with contempt the newspaper accounts of his crime — labeling him an accursed criminal. Feeling misunderstood, he reached for his pocket diary on April 17, 1865, and scribbled, ". . . For six months we had worked to capture. But our cause being almost lost, something decisive & great must be done. But its failure is owing to others who did not strike for their country with a heart. I struck boldly and not as the papers say. . . . Our country owed all her troubles to him, and God simply made me the instrument of his punishment."

Within a few days, Booth's and Herold's horses were starving and moaning. Fearing the horses' noise would bring unwanted visitors to investigate, David Herold walked the horses into the swamp and likely shot them.

The president's funeral was held April 19, 1865. The following day, posters were plastered up and down the East Coast offering $50,000 for the capture of John Wilkes Booth and $25,000 for David Herold. That evening Booth and Herold boarded a small rowboat in which they would cross the Potomac River. But they got lost, and the trip from Maryland into Virginia ended up taking three days.

Once again Booth pulled out his pocket diary and recorded on April 21, 1865:

After being hunted like a dog through swamps, woods, and last night being chased by gun boats till I was forced to return wet cold and starving with every mans (sic) *hand against me, I am here in despair. And why: For doing what Brutus was honored for . . . And yet I for striking down a greater tyrant than they ever knew am looked upon as a common cutthroat. . . . I struck for my country and that alone. A country groaned beneath this tyranny and prayed for this end. Yet now behold the cold hand they extend to me. . . . Tonight I try to escape these blood hounds once more. . . . God's will be done. . . . I have too great a soul to die like a criminal. . . . Oh may he, may he spare me that and let me die bravely.*

On April 23, Booth and Herold finally rowed into Virginia. They moved from place to place, passed from one Confederate agent or sympathizer to the next. Elizabeth Quesenberry, Thomas Harbin, William Bryant, and Dr. Richard Stuart all provided food, transportation, or assistance to the two men, although they sometimes did so grudgingly. They all wanted to get the two as far away as possible quickly so that they themselves did not fall under suspicion. Stuart refused to take in the two men, so they stormed the nearby cabin of Stuart's black servant, William Lucas. Booth threatened Lucas with a knife, demanding he house the two fugitives. William Lucas and his wife surrendered their cabin and slept on the porch, refusing to share a roof with Booth and Herold.

The next morning Booth flashed his gun at Mr. Lucas, thrust $20 at Mrs. Lucas, and demanded their adult son drive them in a wagon to Port Conway. There they met three Confederate soldiers, Mortimer Ruggles, Absalom Bainbridge, and William Jett, to whom David Herold boldly confided their identity. The two were given horses, ferried across the Rappahannock River, and escorted by Jett to Garrett's farm near Port Royal, Virginia.

A BROTHER BURDENED

CHAPTER 9

While one Booth brother lay in hiding, another suffered for his brother's deeds. Mail poured in to Edwin Booth's New York home. First came the many cancellations. Henry C. Jarrett, owner of the theater in which Edwin was currently appearing, wrote:

A fearful calamity is upon us. The President of the United States has fallen by the hand of an assassin, and I am shocked to say suspicion points to one nearly related to you as the perpetrator of this horrid deed. God grant that it may not prove so! Out of respect to the anguish which will fill the public mind . . . I have concluded to close the Boston Theater until further notice.

Anonymous death threats followed in the mail. One such letter read, "You are advised to leave this city and this country forthwith. Your life will be the penalty if you tarry 48 hours longer. Revolvers are already loaded. . . . You are a traitor. . . . We hate the name of Booth."

Finally, Edwin Booth himself spoke through a paid newspaper advertisement that appeared in several cities. "My Fellow Citizens: It has pleased God to lay at the door of my afflicted family the lifeblood of our great, good and martyred President. . . . To you, one and all, go forth our deep, unutterable sympathy; . . . For our present position we are not responsible. For the future — alas; I shall struggle on in my retirement bearing a heavy heart, an oppressed memory and a wounded name — dreadful burdens — to my too welcome grave."

A letter to Edwin's mother, Mary Ann Holmes, arrived at Edwin's house a few days after the assassination. It was from John. In it he begged forgiveness for not writing sooner. The extremely ordinary letter must have stung deeply given the fact it was dated the same day as the assassination, when his heart was set on murder. "Dearest Mother: I know you expect a letter from me, and am sure you will hardly forgive me. But indeed I have nothing to write about. Everything is dull. . . . I only drop you these few lines to let you know I am well. . . . With best love to you all, I am your affectionate son ever, John."

A few days later Holmes' ever-affectionate son John was trapped in Garrett's tobacco barn surrounded by Union troops. During his 12 days on the run, the well-known actor, who limped about wearing only one boot, was recognized by many. The soldiers tracked him down only when he was betrayed by William Jett.

At the farm of Richard Garrett, the soldiers demanded the key to unlock the barn. Then they shoved a terrified John Garrett (Richard's son) into the barn to demand the fugitives surrender. Booth was defiant and threatened him with his gun. After Garrett fled the barn, Colonel Luther Baker shouted his ultimatum. John Wilkes Booth and David Herold had 15 minutes to surrender or he would set fire to the barn and smoke them out. Herold had no intention of being burned alive. He surrendered. But, like a scene from one of his plays, Booth challenged Colonel Baker to a gentleman's duel. He shouted, "I know you to be a brave man and believe you to be honorable: I am a cripple. I have got but one leg. If you will withdraw your men . . . I will come out and fight you."

Baker responded by setting the barn on fire. As the kindling piled along the side of the barn ignited, one of Baker's men, Boston Corbett, watched Booth through a hole in the barn slats just as Booth himself had spied on Lincoln at the theater. As the orange flames roared and danced around him, Booth, clutching a gun and a crutch for his leg, hobbled to the center of the barn. When the fire burst through the roof above him, reaching its fingers out into the inky night, Booth moved toward the door. Boston Corbett held his gun to the knothole and fired.

The bullet pierced John Wilkes Booth in the neck, and he collapsed. Soldiers then carried him out of the burning barn and to Garrett's porch. Booth was paralyzed, but his eyes fluttered and his lips moved. Much like the great president whose life he had cut

A depiction of Booth, who was injured, cold, and hungry as he hid in a tobacco barn, after soldiers set the building on fire. Before the flames could consume him, Booth was shot and dragged out.

short, Booth lay dying in a stranger's home. Twice he croaked, "Tell Mother I die for my country." As the sun rose fully in the morning sky, John Wilkes Booth took his last breath.

When Boston Corbett was asked why he shot Booth, his answer was eerily similar to Booth's reason for shooting Lincoln. "Providence," he said, "directed me."

In the days that followed the assassin's death, his crime cast a long shadow over many of those associated with him. Theater owner John Ford was jailed for 40 days as authorities attempted to find out if he was involved in the plot.

Eight people involved in the plot stood trial for seven weeks in the spring and summer of 1865. David Herold, George Atzerodt, Lewis Powell, and Mary Surratt were sentenced to hang for their crimes. Dr. Samuel Mudd, Michael O'Laughlen, and Samuel Arnold received life sentences. Edmund Spangler was sentenced to six years. O'Laughlen died of yellow fever in prison, but Mudd, Spangler, and Arnold were pardoned by President Johnson in 1869, shortly before he left office.

Upon hearing of his brother's death, Edwin wrote, "At last the terrible end is known — fearful as it is, it is notwithstanding a blessed relief." Now the bearer of an infamous last name, Edwin Booth withdrew from the public eye. He lived amid death threats and the weight of depression. He did not speak the name of his late brother aloud, and he winced at the mention of Lincoln in his presence.

He could not stand retirement, however, for more than a few months. Financial need drove him back to the stage in 1866. He explained his situation to his friend Mrs. Cary by letter. ". . . I have huge debts to pay, a family to care for, a love for the grand and beautiful in art, to boot, to gratify, and hence my sudden resolve to abandon the heavy, aching gloom of my little red room, where I have sat so long chewing my heart in solitude . . ."

Edwin placed two conditions on his return to the stage, vowing never to perform on Good Friday or in Washington, D.C. The name Booth would not be associated with a Washington theater again. Edwin and his brother-in-law, John Clarke, went into business together, purchasing three theaters, one of which his brother Junius ran. One of the plays they produced was *Our American Cousin*, an odd choice given the family history.

While Edwin Booth's professional career took an eventual upswing, his personal life did not. His relationship with Blanche Hanel dissolved, presumably because of the Booth family scandal. His later marriage to Mary McVicker proved unhappy, and she ultimately died in 1881 after a long mental illness.

At his mother's request, Edwin tried to obtain his brother's remains so they could be buried in the family plot. After receiving several denials over four years, a letter to President Andrew Johnson finally resulted in the return of John's body in 1869. He along with Frederick, Elizabeth, Mary Ann, and Henry Byron, his four siblings who had died before him, were buried beside his father's grave.

In 1879 Edwin Booth was himself the victim of an assassination attempt at the theater. A man named Mark Gray fired two shots at Booth as he performed *Richard II* at the McVickers Theater in Chicago. The fact that it was April 23, Shakespeare's birthday, did not escape Booth's notice. He dug one of the bullets out from the theater scenery and engraved it, "From Mark Gray to Edwin Booth, April 23, 1879." He wore it as a good-luck charm on his watch chain.

Edwin Booth ushered in 1889 by opening The Players Club in a remodeled mansion at 16 Gramercy Park in New York City. It was a club for actors, writers, artists, and great thinkers. On the eve of its opening, he

Edwin Booth eventually resumed his acting career in
New York City, where today a statue honoring him stands
in Gramercy Park.

began the New Year's Eve tradition, known as Founders' Night, of standing before the lighted fireplace and passing around his father's silver cup, from which all members drank and toasted The Players' success. The Players Club attracted members such as Mark Twain and General William Sherman, as well as young actors for whom Booth himself paid the membership fee.

On Founders' Night, December 31, 1892, Booth stood before the fireplace with President-elect Grover Cleveland, who made a speech in Edwin's honor. Surely, the words of an American president praising the name of Booth soothed Edwin's wounds 23 years after his brother's notorious crime.

A few months later, on June 7, 1893, Edwin Booth died peacefully in bed in his suite of rooms above The Players Club. He was only 59 years old. Beside his bed stood a framed picture of the brother whose name he no longer spoke.

AFTERWORD

The funeral for Edwin Booth was held June 9, 1893, at the Church of the Transfiguration in New York City. At the same time as Edwin Booth's daughter and friends mourned his passing, a strange event occurred in Washington, D.C. The Records and Pensions Building of the War Department, formerly known as Ford's Theatre, collapsed without warning. Nearly 500 people were inside at the time and dozens were killed or injured.

In 1968 Ford's Theatre was restored as a historical site. Re-created to look just as it did on April 14, 1865, the theater operates both as a modern theater and a museum. Many of the artifacts from the assassination are now housed there.

Edwin Booth's personal rooms atop The Players Club are also frozen in time. His personal belongings are just as they were the night he died. Even the book he was reading is open to the same page. The public rooms below are filled with portraits of Edwin, his father, and other great actors. The small picture on Edwin's bedstand is the only memorial to another Booth, who, before adopting the role of assassin, had been an actor himself.

The presidential box is visible at left in this photograph of the reconstructed Ford's Theatre.

TIMELINE

DECEMBER 2, 1859
John Brown is executed, as witnessed by John Wilkes Booth

NOVEMBER 6, 1860
Abraham Lincoln is elected 16th president

DECEMBER 20, 1860
South Carolina secedes from the Union

FEBRUARY 1861
The Confederate States of America forms;
Jefferson Davis is named its president

APRIL 12, 1861
Fort Sumter is fired upon, beginning the Civil War

MARCH 1863
Lincoln sees Edwin Booth perform Shakespeare's *Hamlet*

JULY 1-3, 1863
Battle of Gettysburg

JULY 13, 1863
Edwin and John witness the New York Draft Riots
outside Edwin's home

NOVEMBER 9, 1863
Lincoln sees John Wilkes Booth perform in *The Marble Heart*

SEPTEMBER 2, 1864
Atlanta falls to the North

OCTOBER 18, 1864
John Wilkes Booth travels to Canada

NOVEMBER 8, 1864
Edwin Booth votes for Lincoln, who is elected to a second term

NOVEMBER 25, 1864
The Booth brothers perform Shakespeare's *Julius Caesar*;
Confederates start fires in New York

NOVEMBER 26, 1864
Edwin Booth throws John Wilkes Booth out of his house and begins 100 nights of *Hamlet*

JANUARY 31, 1865
Congress passes the 13th Amendment, outlawing slavery

MARCH 4, 1865
John Wilkes Booth attends Lincoln's second inauguration and, possibly, the inaugural ball

MARCH 17, 1865
John Wilkes Booth and conspirators fail in an attempt to kidnap Lincoln

APRIL 9, 1865
Robert E. Lee surrenders to Ulysses S. Grant at Appomattox

APRIL 11, 1865
John Wilkes Booth sees Lincoln's address during Illumination Night celebrations

APRIL 14, 1865
John Wilkes Booth shoots Lincoln at Ford's Theatre

APRIL 15, 1865
Lincoln dies; Andrew Johnson becomes 17th president

APRIL 26, 1865
John Wilkes Booth dies from a gunshot wound

JULY 7, 1865
Four of John Wilkes Booth's conspirators are executed

DECEMBER 31, 1888
Edwin Booth opens The Players Club

DECEMBER 31, 1892
President-elect Grover Cleveland honors Edwin Booth

JUNE 7, 1893
Edwin Booth dies

DERINGER GUN
KNIFE & SHEATH

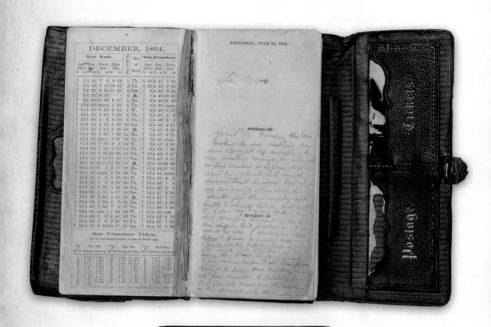

BOOTH'S DIARY

COMPASS

BOOTH CONSPIRATORS

LEWIS POWELL

MARY SURRATT

DAVID E. HEROLD

GEORGE A. ATZERODT

GLOSSARY

abolitionist — a person who supported the banning of slavery

armory — a place where weapons are stored

blockade — a military effort to keep goods from entering and leaving a region

chloroform — a toxic liquid once used to ease pain or make a person unconscious

divisive — creating division or disagreement

emancipation — freeing someone from the control of another

gallows — a wooden frame used for hanging criminals

greasepaint — an oily type of makeup used by stage actors

heinous — hateful and wicked

militia — groups of volunteer citizens organized to fight but who are not professional soldiers

musket — a gun with a long barrel that was used before the rifle was invented

providence — determined by God or under God's care

resolution — a statement or expression of opinion, usually voted on by a legislature, board, or other group

tragedian — an actor known for performing tragic roles

treasonous — disloyal and likely to undermine a government or cause harm to its leader

Underground Railroad — a system of helpful people and safe places for runaway slaves during the mid-1800s

valet — a servant who attends to the personal needs of another person

vigilante — a person who punishes others personally and illegally rather than relying on legal authorities

INTERNET SITES

Use FactHound to find Internet sites related to this book.

Visit www.facthound.com

Just type in 9781515773382 and go.

READ MORE

Fitzgerald, Stephanie. *A Civil War Timeline*. North Mankato, Minn.: Capstone Press, 2014.

Samuels, Charlie. *The Attack on Fort Sumter*. New York, Gareth Stevens Publishing, 2014.

Swanson, James L. *Chasing Lincoln's Killer*. New York: Scholastic Press, 2009.

SELECT BIBLIOGRAPHY

Booth, John Wilkes. *Right or Wrong, God Judge Me: The Writings of John Wilkes Booth*. Edited by John Rhodehamel. Champaign, Ill.: University of Illinois Press, 1997.

Clarke, Asia Booth, and Terry Alford. *John Wilkes Booth: A Sister's Memoir*. Jackson, Miss.: University Press of Mississippi, 1996.

Ferguson, W. J. *I Saw Booth Shoot Lincoln*. Boston: Houghton Mifflin Company, 1930.

Grossman, Edwina Booth. *Edwin Booth: Recollections by His Daughter Edwina Booth Grossman and Letters*. Charleston, South Carolina: BiblioBazaar, 2009.

Lockridge, Richard. *Darling of Misfortune, Edwin Booth: 1833–1893*. London: The Century Co., 1932.

Matthews, Brander, and Laurence Hutton. *The Life and Art of Edwin Booth and His Contemporaries*. Boston: Page, 1886.

Pitman, Benn, comp. *The Assassination of President Lincoln and the Trial of Conspirators*. CreateSpace, 2012.

Power-Waters, Alma. *The Story of Young Edwin Booth*. New York: Dutton, 1955.

Smith, Gene. *American Gothic: The Story of America's Legendary Theatrical Family, Junius, Edwin, and John Wilkes Booth*. New York: Simon & Schuster, 1992.

Swanson, James L. *Manhunt: The 12-Day Chase for Lincoln's Killer*. New York: William Morrow, 2006.

Titone, Nora. *My Thoughts Be Bloody: The Bitter Rivalry Between Edwin and John Wilkes Booth That Led to an American Tragedy*. New York: Free Press, 2010.

Townsend, George Alfred. *Life, Crime and Capture of John Wilkes Booth*. CreateSpace, 2015.

SOURCE NOTES

Page 16, "Amongst them I notice Mr. J. Wilkes Booth . . ." Gene Smith. *American Gothic: The Story of America's Legendary Theatrical Family: Junius, Edwin, and John Wilkes Booth*. New York: Simon & Schuster, 1992, pp. 79–80.

Page 16, "Your news concerning the mad step . . ." Ibid., p. 80.

Page 18, "In every word and every gesture . . ." Nora Titone. *My Thoughts Be Bloody: The Bitter Rivalry Between Edwin and John Wilkes Booth That Led to an American Tragedy*. New York: Free Press, 2010, p. 200.

Page 19, "I saw John Brown hung . . ." John Wilkes Booth. *Right or Wrong, God Judge Me: The Writings of John Wilkes Booth*. Edited by John Rhodehamel. Champaign, Ill.: University of Illinois Press, 1997, p. 60.

Page 19–21, "I, John Brown, am now quite certain . . ." "John Brown." History.com. http://www.history.com/topics/john-brown

Page 27, "In your hand, my fellow countrymen, and not in mine . . ." "Lincoln Inaugurated." History.com, http://www.history.com/this-day-in-history/lincoln-inaugurated

Pages 27–28, ". . . an ardent lover of the South and her policy . . ." Asia Booth Clarke and Terry Alford. *John Wilkes Booth: A Sister's Memoir*. Jackson, Miss.: University Press of Mississippi, 1996, p. 83.

Page 28, "He (John) felt it rather premature that Edwin should . . ." Ibid., p. 80.

Page 33, "At an early age my memory . . ." Nora Titone. *My Thoughts Be Bloody: The Bitter Rivalry Between Edwin and John Wilkes Booth That Led to an American Tragedy*. New York: Free Press, 2010., p. 90.

Page 36, "As Pescara . . ." *The Baltimore Sun*, Baltimore. 19 March 1863.

Page 37, "Mr. Edwin Booth, it is known, is a young man who . . ." *The Cincinnati Daily Press*. 12 November 1861.

Page 41, "What a glorious opportunity there is for a man . . ." Nora Titone. *My Thoughts Be Bloody: The Bitter Rivalry Between Edwin and John Wilkes Booth That Led to an American Tragedy*. New York: Free Press, 2010, p. 275.

Page 46, "My soul, life and possessions . . ." Asia Booth Clarke and Terry Alford. *John Wilkes Booth: A Sister's Memoir*. Jackson, Miss.: University Press of Mississippi, 1996, p. 82.

Page 46, "My brains are worth twenty men . . ." Ibid., p. 82.

Page 46, "I am he, if to be a doctor means . . ." Ibid., p. 83.

Page 46, "... horse-collars and so forth . . ." Ibid., p. 83.

Page 51, "John sat up all Monday night . . ." Ibid., p. 86.

Page 52, "That was a close call . . ." Gene Smith. *American Gothic: The Story of America's Legendary Theatrical Family: Junius, Edwin, and John Wilkes Booth*. New York: Simon & Schuster, 1992, p. 103.

Page 56, "I voted (for Lincoln) t' other day . . ." Edwina Booth Grossman. *Edwin Booth: Recollections by His Daughter Edwina Booth Grossman and Letters*. Charleston, South Carolina: BiblioBazaar, 2009, p. 155.

Page 56, "On Friday, the 25th, without fail, the long-talked-of benefit . . ." Ibid., pp. 154–155.

Page 57, "... Owing to the generous zeal and untiring devotion of Mr. Edwin Booth . . ." *The New York Times.* 25 November 1864.

Page 62, "What an excellent chance I had . . ." John Wilkes Booth. *Right or Wrong, God Judge Me: The Writings of John Wilkes Booth.* Edited by John Rhodehamel. Champaign, Ill.: University of Illinois Press, 1997, p. 14.

Page 65, "That is the last speech he will . . ." James L. Swanson. *Manhunt: The 12-day Chase for Lincoln's Killer.* New York: William Morrow, 2006, p. 6.

Page 68, "To My Countrymen: For years I have devoted my time . . ." John Wilkes Booth. *Right or Wrong, God Judge Me: The Writings of John Wilkes Booth.* Edited by John Rhodehamel. Champaign, Ill.: University of Illinois Press, 1997, p. 149–150.

Page 69, "When Caesar had conquered the enemies of Rome . . ." Ibid., pp. 149–150.

Page 70, "Don't wish to disturb you . . ." Ibid, p. 146.

Page 77 "Sic semper tyrannis" Gene Smith. *American Gothic: The Story of America's Legendary Theatrical Family: Junius, Edwin, and John Wilkes Booth.* New York: Simon & Schuster, 1992, p. 154.

Page 77 "The South is avenged." Swanson, James L. *Manhunt: The 12-day Chase for Lincoln's Killer.* New York: William Morrow, 2006, p. 48.

Page 77 "Stop that man!" Ibid., p. 49.

Page 77 "He has shot the President." Ibid., p. 49.

Page 79, "Order, order! Keep your places!" Gene Smith. *American Gothic: The Story of America's Legendary Theatrical Family: Junius, Edwin, and John Wilkes Booth.* New York: Simon & Schuster, 1992, p. 155.

Page 80, "His wound is mortal." Ibid., p. 158.

Pages 84–85, "For six months we had worked to capture . . ." John Wilkes Booth. *Right or Wrong, God Judge Me. The Writings of John Wilkes Booth.* Edited by John Rhodehamel. Champaign, Ill.: University of Illinois Press, 1997, p. 154.

Pages 85–86, "After being hunted like a dog . . ." Ibid., pp. 154–155.

Page 89, "A fearful calamity is upon us . . ." Gene Smith. *American Gothic: The Story of America's Legendary Theatrical Family: Junius, Edwin, and John Wilkes Booth.* New York: Simon & Schuster, 1992, p. 177.

Page 90, "You are advised to leave this city . . ." Ibid., p. 181.

Page 90, "My Fellow Citizens . . ." Ibid., pp. 181-182.

Page 91, "Dearest Mother: I know you expect . . ." John Wilkes Booth. *Right or Wrong, God Judge Me: The Writings of John Wilkes Booth.* Edited by John Rhodehamel. Champaign, Ill.: University of Illinois Press, 1997, p. 144.

Page 92, "I know you to be a brave man ..." James L. Swanson. *Manhunt: The 12-day Chase for Lincoln's Killer.* New York: William Morrow, 2006, p. 331.

Page 94, "Tell mother I die . . ." Ibid., p. 337.

Page 94 "Providence . . ." Ibid., p. 341.

Page 95, "At last the terrible end is known . . ." Asia Booth Clarke and Terry Alford. *John Wilkes Booth: A Sister's Memoir.* Jackson, Miss.: University Press of Mississippi, 1996.

Page 95, ". . . I have huge debts . . ." Edwina Booth Grossman. *Edwin Booth: Recollections by His Daughter Edwina Booth Grossman and Letters.* Charleston, South Carolina: BiblioBazaar, 2009, pp. 174–175.

INDEX